KOREAN SCRIPT HACKING
The optimal pathway to learn the Korean alphabet

T0349792

Teach Yourself®

KOREAN SCRIPT HACKING
The optimal pathway to learn the Korean alphabet

Developed with an algorithm that guarantees the most efficient route to success

Judith Meyer

First published in Great Britain in 2019 by Hodder and Stoughton. An Hachette UK company.

Copyright © Judith Meyer 2019

The right of Judith Meyer to be identified as the Author of the Work has been asserted by them in accordance with the Copyright, Designs and Patents Act 1988.

Database right Hodder & Stoughton (makers)

The Teach Yourself name is a registered trademark of Hachette UK.

British Library Cataloguing in Publication Data: a catalogue record for this title is available from the British Library.

Library of Congress Catalog Card Number: on file.

978 1 473 67977 1

4

Typeset by Integra Software Services Pvt. Ltd., Pondicherry, India.

Printed and bound in Great Britain by Clays Ltd, Elcograf S.p.A.

John Murray Learning policy is to use papers that are natural, renewable and recyclable products and made from wood grown in sustainable forests. The logging and manufacturing processes are expected to conform to the environmental regulations of the country of origin.

Carmelite House
50 Victoria Embankment
London EC4Y 0DZ
www.hodder.co.uk

CONTENTS

Dedication   6

A note from Judith   7

Introduction to the script and transliteration   8

Alphabet   10

How to use this course   13

    1 First letters   15

    2 M-O-R-E letters   25

    3 Flat land and mountains   34

    4 G and vowels with Y and W   46

    5 Last consonants   59

    6 Different writing styles   71

Answer key   112

Phrasebook   126

Dedicated to my family, who supported me in my love of languages despite not seeing the fascination.

A NOTE FROM JUDITH

Despite having learnt a number of languages to an advanced level, I often had great difficulty memorizing things. I always looked for shortcuts, tips, tricks and techniques to make learning that little bit easier. Some of this was probably overkill, but when it comes to my method for learning scripts however, I am convinced that I hit gold.

Letters are introduced one at a time alongside a lot of fun, puzzle-based reading practice, which helps you to learn the new letter effortlessly, and to review those you already know at the same time. Unlike other courses, which often provide a list of all letters of a new alphabet and encourage you to learn them ahead of the first lesson, *Script Hacking* focuses solely on the letters themselves, so you can use it as a foundation for future study or for a fast, effective overview of the basics.

I don't go into Korean grammar – there are other courses for that – or even word usage. I ignore controversies and dialects. I also don't claim to be an expert about the Korean language (just an expert on learning writing systems) – that's why I worked with native speakers and teachers of Korean; without them, this course would not have been possible.

This course was one of the first I created when I invented the algorithm that underpins the *Script Hacking* method. I developed a course prototype, an experiment, for Korean and put it on my website – and the amazing feedback from visitors convinced me that the method was worth using, perfecting, and eventually turning into the course you're holding in your hands now.

I am grateful to everyone who sent me feedback over the years I ran this experiment. Without this feedback, your learning experience wouldn't be nearly as smooth. Also, I would like to thank Emma Green, who saw this method and believed in it enough to convince John Murray Learning to publish it within the Teach Yourself series.

Judith Meyer

INTRODUCTION TO THE SCRIPT AND TRANSLITERATION

The Korean alphabet was invented by King Sejong the Great in the 15th century. Until then, Korean had mostly been written in Chinese characters, otherwise known as Hanja, which weren't however well-suited to the language (Korean and Chinese belong to different language families). The Korean alphabet, also known as Hangul, was thus invented in order to improve literacy levels, as people at that time found the thousands of characters difficult to learn; unlike others, this alphabet did not evolve naturally and was constructed. Hangul was not immediately adopted by the entire society, and knowing Hanja was necessary to be able to read literature (in South Korea) even as late as the 1970s. Now, however, Hangul has almost completely replaced Chinese characters.

This is the word *Hanja* written in Hangul (left) and in Hanja (right):

한자   漢字

For a beginner learner of an Asian language, it may initially seem difficult to distinguish Korean from Chinese and from Japanese, but with a bit of practice the distinction becomes impossible to un-see. The reason is that Korean script may, to the untrained eye, look like characters, but that is an illusion; what looks like a character is actually a box full of letters. Each 'box' contains the letters for one syllable. For example, the word *Hanja* consists of two syllables / two 'boxes':

한 and 자

The first syllable contains three letters: ㅎ, ㅏ and ㄴ, that is **H, A** and **N**. Have a look at how these individual letters have been arranged so as to fill an imaginary square box. The second syllable contains only two letters: ㅈ and ㅏ, that is **J**, and then **A** again. It is key to the Korean writing system that every syllable fits into an imaginary square box of equal size, independent of whether there are two, three or in some cases even four letters inside it. The letters must grow or shrink accordingly. Sometimes they also connect or deform a bit, just as our letters do in cursive (handwritten) script. For example, ㄴ and ㅏ together look like 나.

The consonants of the Korean script have a variety of shapes, intended to be reminiscent of the shape that the tongue, teeth, palate and throat take as they articulate the sound. This is how you can tell that the alphabet was created on a drawing board and didn't evolve naturally. The vowels are all based on three elements: a horizontal line representing the earth, a dot or short line representing the sun, and a vertical line representing the upright human as a mediator between the two.

In practice, the simple vowels all consist of one long line and possibly a short line on it. Depending on whether the long line is horizontal or vertical, that is, depending on whether the vowel as a whole is rather tall or rather wide, the placement of letters inside the imaginary square box has to be adjusted. If the vowel (which always comes in second place) is tall, then the consonant is placed on the left and the vowel on the right, as in 나. If the vowel is wide, then the arrangement necessarily has to be a top-down one, like 느 , because otherwise the squareness of the syllable couldn't be guaranteed. In any case, final consonants are placed underneath, as in 한 .

Korean letters don't correspond exactly to English letters. While Korean spelling is largely straightforward, Korean has some sounds or distinctions that English lacks. For example, there are three different consonants that all sound similar to **K**. When transliterating them (writing Korean with Latin letters, for the purpose here of allowing you to check the answers to the exercises), this course will use **g** for one, **k** for another, and **kk** for the third, even if they don't exactly sound like **g** / **k** / **kk** (use the recordings in order to perfect your pronunciation). This is in line with the system known as 'Revised Romanization', the official transliteration system in South Korea. Whenever you come across transliterated Korean, e.g. on subway signs or online, it will use this Revised Romanization, so knowing the system is useful beyond this course.

ALPHABET

The Korean alphabet consists of 19 consonants and 21 vowels. Here they are presented in the modern order and with the transliteration used in South Korea. North Korea uses a different order and different transliteration.

Consonants

Korean letter	Transliteration	Name
ㄱ	g	Giyeok
ㄲ	kk	Ssang Giyeok
ㄴ	n	Nieun
ㄷ	d	Digeut
ㄸ	tt	Ssang Digeut
ㄹ	r / l	Rieul
ㅁ	m	Mieum
ㅂ	b	Bieup
ㅃ	pp	Ssang Bieup
ㅅ	s	Siot
ㅆ	ss	Ssang Siot
ㅇ	ng	Ieung

Korean letter	Transliteration	Name
ㅈ	j	Jieut
ㅉ	jj	Ssang Jieut
ㅊ	ch	Chieut
ㅋ	k	Kieuk
ㅌ	t	Tieut
ㅍ	p	Pieup
ㅎ	h	Hieut

◁)) **01.01** Listen to the audio to hear how the letters are pronounced.

LANGUAGE TIP

Look at the letters and notice that many are variations of previous letters, for example the **Ssang** letter looks like a doubled version of the previous letter.

Vowels

Korean letter	Transliteration	Korean letter	Transliteration
ㅏ	a	ㅚ	oe
ㅐ	ae	ㅛ	yo
ㅑ	ya	ㅜ	u
ㅒ	yae	ㅝ	wo
ㅓ	eo	ㅞ	we
ㅔ	e	ㅟ	wi
ㅕ	yeo	ㅠ	yu
ㅖ	ye	ㅡ	eu
ㅗ	o	ㅢ	ui
ㅘ	wa	ㅣ	i
ㅙ	wae		

For vowels, the transliteration is also the name of the letter.

◁)) **01.02 Listen to the audio to hear how the letters are pronounced.**

> **LANGUAGE TIP**
>
> Look at the letters and notice that there are only a few basic vowels
> and then a lot of diphthongs (complex vowel sounds) or versions of
> the same vowel with **Y** or **W** in front. Since the Korean alphabet is a
> constructed one, the sound patterns are matched in the shape of the
> letters; in fact the shape of vowels is predictable.

HOW TO USE THIS COURSE

This course was created with the help of a cutting-edge computer algorithm that identified the optimal order to introduce the letters of the alphabet. Every section has been designed to build on top of the previous ones. Therefore it is important to study this course in a linear fashion rather than jumping back and forth.

Every section starts with a new letter. Look at it carefully and copy it down. Letters should be written from left to right and then top to bottom, as in English. Once a Korean letter is introduced, it is also shown in syllable boxes, that is, in combination with other letters that you have already met in the course, so you should copy both the single letter and the examples given with other letter combinations. There is space to copy the letters inside the book, but feel free to also copy the letters into an exercise book, especially if you are finding one of the letters more difficult to write than the others. You might even want to copy every Korean word in this course and later all the texts from your lessons. Copying Korean will help you to get used to writing the letters and also to improve your handwriting.

After copying the letter, you will be asked to find the letter in a short Korean text. This will increase your familiarity with it and will train your eyes to process Korean text more quickly, especially as the Korean way of placing the letters inside imaginary boxes is completely different from how letters are placed in English, or even Russian or Greek, for example.

Next comes the core of the method: exercises where you have to read or write Korean words. These are real Korean words but they have been carefully chosen for their similarity to English. If you don't understand a word immediately, say it out loud or write down the transliteration and see if it sounds or looks familiar. The reason this method starts with such words is that it's much easier to learn the letters when you don't have to simultaneously learn new vocabulary. When children learn the alphabet at school, they also start by learning to read familiar words in their native language. Indeed, learning the alphabet is the foundation for learning everything else.

As you can see on the Alphabet pages, the transliteration (the way to render a Korean letter in the Latin alphabet, as used in the English language) is often obvious. For example, Korean has a letter that is pronounced just like **M**, so the transliteration will also be **M**. Whenever there is no obvious link between the sound and a letter in the Latin alphabet, the lesson will tell you which Latin letter or letter combination has been chosen to render a given Korean letter.

Answers are provided in the Answer key at the end of this course, and you can listen to the sounds of the letters at library.teachyourself.com. There are also pages after the lessons to practice writing the letters in the script. Throughout the course, you will find #ScriptHacks to help you remember the letter and useful learning tips to help you to learn the language.

Take as long as you need for this course. Some have completed it in a few hours; others have taken weeks, studying it more thoroughly and retaining more. The course has been divided into several lessons with review sections to help you to find good places to stop for the day, but you can continue for as long as you want. In the end, what matters is that you become comfortable with the Korean script and have fun doing so! Good luck.

Icons

 Writing

📖 Reading

🔍 Spot the letter

◁)) Listening

🔤 Script hack

1 FIRST LETTERS

Bieup ㅂ

As you may have guessed from the name, **Bieup** is the Korean equivalent of the English letter

 #ScriptHack

To associate the picture and the sound, think of **Bieup** as a **b**ucket.

B. At the beginning of a syllable it sounds more like **B** (though some may perceive it as **P**) and at the end of a syllable it sounds more like **P**. That is why the letter name **Bieup**, which is spelt in Korean with a **Bieup** at the beginning and end, has a **B** at the beginning and a **P** at the end. In transliteration, note down **b** when **Bieup** is at the beginning of a syllable and **p** when it is at the end.

✏ **1 Practise writing Bieup.**

ㅂ						

 #ScriptHack

When writing, ensure that you stay within imaginary squares, but try to fill them well – don't have letters clinging to one of the corners.

🔍 **2 Find the five Bieups in the following paragraph. Keep in mind that Bieup may have lines from adjacent vowels touching it.**

저는 인도네시아, 베트남,
중국, 한국, 그리고 일본이
정말 즐거웠습니다.
일본 스시와 차는 정말
맛있었습니다!

LANGUAGE TIP

This will take time at first, but soon you'll develop a feel for the Korean script and the way letters are hiding within it.

A ㅏ

This Korean vowel sounds similar to the English **A**. The vertical line of ㅏ was originally supposed to represent the concept of a human, and the short line or dot was originally supposed to represent the sun, so one might say that ㅏ is a human with the sun on the right side.

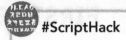

#ScriptHack

To remember this letter, associate ㅏ with the picture of an **a**nchor.

 3 Practise writing A.

In order to combine **Bieup** and **A** into the Korean word **ba**, all you have to do is to try to fit them into an imaginary square box. This is done by writing the letter ㅏ next to ㅂ, like this:

바

This incidentally is the Korean word for *bar*. When a syllable ends in a consonant, the final consonant is always placed underneath the rest of the letters in the syllable box. For example, this is how to write the Korean word **bap**:

밥

Note how the shape of **Bieup** had to be adjusted to fit underneath **ba**. Each syllable always gets one box, and the letters must fill it as well as possible.

✏ 4 Practise writing **ba** and **bap**.

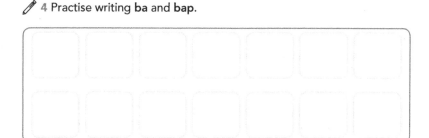

🔍 5 Find the four **As** in the following paragraph.

저는 인도네시아, 중국, 한국, 그리고 일본이
정말 즐거웠습니다.

LANGUAGE TIP

If you see letters that look like ㅏ but with the line on the wrong side, or
with a double vertical line, they are different vowels.

Rieul ㄹ

This letter sounds a little like
the English letter **R** or **L**. At the
beginning of a syllable it sounds
more like **R**, and at the end it
sounds more like **L**, as can be

 #ScriptHack

In order to remember the shape
of this letter and associate it with
the sound, think of **Rieul** as a
winding **r**oad.

gathered from the letter's name in Korean (which is spelled with a **Rieul** at
the beginning and end). This is a common pattern for Korean consonants
– their names start and end with the letter in question, so you know how
a letter is pronounced at the beginning and at the end of a syllable just
by remembering its name. Also note that **Rieul** is transliterated as **r** at the
beginning of a syllable and as **l** at the end, to reflect the slight difference in
pronunciation. Despite this, **Rieul** is also used to represent an initial **l** at the
beginning of foreign names – there simply is no other suitable letter.

✏ **6** Practise writing **Rieul**.

ㄹ					

🔍 **7** Find the six **Rieuls** in the following paragraph.

저는 인도네시아, 베트남, 중국, 한국, 그리고
일본이 정말 즐거웠습니다. 일본 스시와 차는
정말 맛있었습니다!

📖 **8** The following is a female name. Read the Korean letters and work
out which name it is:

🔊 **01.03**

바바라

ㅣ ㅣ

This is the equivalent of the English
letter **I** in Korean. Here are some
examples of how it looks combined
with **Bieup** and **Rieul**. Remember that
Rieul is used for both the **L** and **R** sounds in Korean.

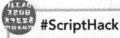

#ScriptHack

The Korean letter **I** looks like a
capital **I** in English.

ㅣ	비	리	빌		

✏️ **9** Practise writing I on its own and in combination with other letters.

<table>
<tr><td></td><td></td><td></td><td></td><td></td></tr>
<tr><td></td><td></td><td></td><td></td><td></td></tr>
</table>

🔍 **10** Find the ten Is in the following paragraph.

저는 인도네시아, 베트남, 중국,  **#ScriptHack**
한국, 그리고 일본이 정말
즐거웠습니다. 일본 스시와
차는 정말 맛있었습니다!

Only a single vertical line is I. If there is more than one line, it's a different vowel.

📖 **11** Read the Korean letters and use the clues to work out the meaning of the following words.

🔊 01.04

    a Male names: 빌 and 빌리
    b Currency: 리라
    c French city: 릴

All Korean syllables have to start with a consonant, so you cannot write

ㅏㅂ or ㅏㄹ, for example.

For syllables that start with a vowel, there is a special convention.

leung O

This letter is used as a placeholder silent letter for syllables that start with a vowel. It will be completely

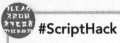

#ScriptHack

leung has zero sound, so it looks like a big zero.

inaudible (and also not transliterated) at the beginning of a syllable. We'll cover **leung** at the end of a syllable later on.

This is how to write the expression **ah!**

아

This is how to write **ih.**

이

And this is how to write **al** – the final consonant will always have to fit underneath the rest of the syllable.

알

O	아	이	알			

✏ 12 Practise writing **leung, ah, ih** and **al.**

🔍 **13** Find the twelve **leungs** in the following paragraph.

저는 인도네시아, 베트남, 중국, 한국, 그리고
일본이 정말 즐거웠습니다. 일본 스시와 차는
정말 맛있었습니다!

LANGUAGE TIP

Normally all circles should be **leung**, except ㅎ – that's the letter **Hieut**, which you'll learn later. Also, if you see a letter that looks similar but is not rounded (ㅁ), that's the letter **Mieum**.

📖 **14** Read the Korean letters and use the clues to work out the meaning of the following words.

🔊 **01.05**

a Swedish band: 아바

b Arab country on the Mediterranean: 리비아

c Name of a famous boxer: 알리

Nieun ㄴ

This is the equivalent of the letter **N** in Korean – pronounced as **N** both at the beginning and at the end of syllables. There is just

#ScriptHack

Think of **Nieun** as a nose you might draw in a caricature to help remember this letter.

one additional point to remember: the combination **Bieup-Nieun**, which is extremely common in Korean, is not pronounced *pn* but *mn* due to assimilation. For example, the Korean word for *please*, in which **Nieun** follows **Bieup**, is **butakhamnida**, not **butakhapnida**. In the Korean alphabet it is written as: 부탁합니다.

This is **Nieun** in combination with some of the letters you have learnt.

LANGUAGE TIP

When one syllable ends in a consonant and the next syllable starts with a consonant, their pronunciation will adjust in order to make the word easier to pronounce. Linguists call this assimilation. This course will not explain all possible assimilation patterns; you'll hear them for yourself.

🖊 **15** Practise writing **Nieun** on its own and in combination with other letters.

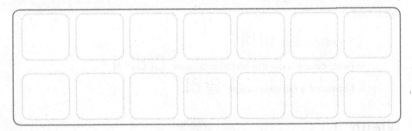

When you write the syllable **na** by placing **Nieun** and **A** into an imaginary square box, it may look like this:

나

Nieun is slightly crooked here, and taller than it is wide, because of the need to fit **A** next to it and still stay within the space of the (imaginary) square box. Alternatively, **Nieun** may become quite a bit more crooked and flow into **A**, like this:

나

This depends on the writer or the font. The former example is used throughout this course, because it is easier to read.

🔍 16 Find the twelve **Nieuns** in the following paragraph.

저는 인도네시아, 베트남, 중국, 한국, 그리고
일본이 정말 즐거웠습니다. 일본 스시와 차는
정말 맛있었습니다!

📖 17 Read the Korean letters and use the clues to work out the meaning
of the following words.

🔊 01.06

a A fruit: 바나나

b Two names: 안나 and 닐

c Two countries: 이란 and 알바니아

d A Spanish-speaking city: 아바나

e Capital of Austria: 빈

f A flavour: 바닐라

LANGUAGE TIP

Bieup can replace
V as well as B in
foreign words,
because Korean
does not have a V.

REVIEW

You've come a long way! Here are all the letters you have learnt so far:

ㅂ	ㅏ	ㄹ	ㅣ	ㅇ	ㄴ

✏️ **1** Copy the letters and write the letter names underneath them.

📖 **2** Transliterate the following Korean words.

Korean	Transliteration	Meaning
알	_____	*egg*
비	_____	*rain*
반	_____	*half*

2 M-O-R-E LETTERS

Mieum ☐

This is the equivalent of the letter **M** in Korean. It is shown here in its simple form and then in some letter combinations.

#ScriptHack

To remember the shape, think of **Mieum** as a mouth opened as wide as possible in astonishment.

| ☐ | 아 | 이 | 밈 | | |

✏️ 1 Practise writing **Mieum**.

🔍 2 Find the four **Mieums** in the following paragraph.

저는 인도네시아, 베트남, 중국, 한국, 그리고 일본이 정말 즐거웠습니다. 일본 스시와 차는 정말 맛있었습니다!

#ScriptHack

Here's how to tell **Mieum** and **Ieung** (○) apart: **Ieung** is a circle or at least an elongated rounded shape, while **Mieum** always has corners.

📖 3 Read the Korean letters and use the clues to work out the meaning of the following words.

🔊 02.01

    a Woman's name: 마리아

    b Countries in Africa: 나미비아 – 말리

    c Capitals of Arab countries: 암만 – 마나마

    d Other capitals: 마닐라 – 리마

    e Name of Vietnam before it became Vietnam: 안남

    f Distance measurement: 마일

    g Famous singer: 밥 말리

ㅗ

This is the equivalent of the letter **O** in Korean. The long horizontal line represents the earth, and the dot / short line above it is the sun.

> **#ScriptHack**
>
> Imagine **O** as representing the 'h**o**riz**o**n' to remember this letter.

O is the first example of a class of vowels that are wider rather than tall. As you saw, the Korean letters **A** and **I** are rather tall, so they are placed to the right of the initial consonant. The Korean letter **O**, and others like it, are too wide for that to work, so they are placed underneath the initial consonant. Final consonants will still go below, as shown in the following examples.

ㅗ	보	노	론	몰		

✏️ **4** Practise writing **O** on its own and in combination with other letters.

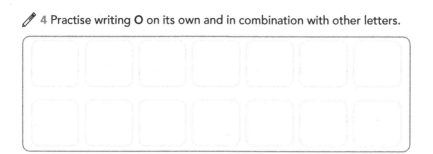

🔍 **5** Find the ten **Os** in the following paragraph.

뉴욕, 뉴햄프셔, 매사추세츠, 뉴저지,
버지니아, 테네시, 아칸소, 오클라호마,
뉴멕시코, 콜로라도, 유타, 아이다호 및
오레곤.

📖 **6** Read the Korean letters and use the clues to work out the meaning of the following words.

🔊 **02.02**

    a Names: 나오미 – 노아

    b Cities in Europe: 로마 – 밀라노 – 본

    c City in Africa: 나이로비

    d An American state: 일리노이

    e Countries: 볼리비아 – 오만

    f The Korean word for Japan: 일본

    g A musical instrument: 바이올린

Kieuk ㅋ

This letter is the Korean equivalent of **K**. It is aspirated (pronounced with a puff of air), just like the

 #ScriptHack

In order to remember the shape and associate it with the sound, think of **Kieuk** as an old-style key.

English **K**. In Korean, aspiration is important, because there are equivalent consonants without aspiration. The unaspirated equivalent of **Kieuk**, which you'll learn later, is **Giyeok**, written as ㄱ. **Kieuk** ㅋ and **Giyeok** ㄱ differ only by one additional line. Watch out for these doubled lines in other aspirated consonants.

Like **Nieun**, **Kieuk** will bend a bit when necessary; when combined with a tall vowel it may even start to resemble a **3** as shown in the examples below.

ㅋ	코	카	킨			

✎ **7** Practise writing **Kieuk** on its own and in combination with other letters.

🔍 **8** Find the four **Kieuks** in the following paragraph.

뉴욕, 뉴햄프셔, 매사추세츠, 뉴저지, 버지니아,
테네시, 아칸소, 오클라호마, 뉴멕시코,
콜로라도, 유타, 아이다호 및 오레곤.

📖 **9** Read the Korean letters and use the clues to work out the meaning of the following words.

◁)) **02.03**

a Name: 킴

b Countries: 모로코 – 모나코 – 콜롬비아 –
코모로

c Cities: 카이로 – 콜롬보 – 마카오

d Brands: 노키아 – 코카콜라

e Words Korean borrowed from English: 아이콘 – 코코아 – 킬로 – 알코올

Tieut ㅌ

This is the equivalent of the letter **T** in Korean. It is aspirated (pronounced with a puff of air) like its English equivalent, and in Korean that means that it's written with one more line than its unaspirated equivalent **Digeut** ㄷ, which you'll learn later. Here Tieut is also shown in combination with other letters.

 #ScriptHack

In order to remember the shape and associate it with the sound, think of **Tieut** as a mouth (missing the right side) with two rows of white teeth visible.

| ㅌ | 타 | 티 | 도 | 톨 | | |

🖉 **10** Practise writing **Tieut** on its own and in combination with other letters.

🔍 **11** Find the four **Tieuts** in the following paragraph.

그리고 톨스토이, 셰익스피어, 괴테, 쉴러, 칼
마르크스에 대해 배웠습니다. 또한 모차르트,
바흐, 차이코프스키를 들었습니다.

📖 **12** Read the Korean letters and use the clues to work out the meaning
of the following words.

◁》 **02.04**

a Names: 톰 – 토니 – 마틴
b Cities: 토론토 – 키토 – 콜카타 – 탈린 –
알마티 – 토리노 – 안타나나리보
c Countries: 이탈리아 – 몰타 – 아이티 –
모리타니
d Food: 타코
e Contained in food: 비타민

E ㅔ

This is the equivalent of the letter **E**
as in bed. It consists of two vertical
lines (based on the original concept
of humans) and a short line (based on
the original concept of the sun)
on the left. Here **E** is also shown in
combination with other letters.

#ScriptHack

The Korean letter **E** looks like a
two-lane road with a turnoff on
the left – **E** is for left.

ㅔ	베	네	렌	케	

✏️ **13** Practise writing **E** on its own and in combination with other letters.

🔍 **14** Find the five **Es** in the following paragraph.

많은 주들을 봤습니다: 뉴욕, 뉴햄프셔,
매사추세츠, 뉴저지, 버지니아, 테네시,
아칸소, 오클라호마, 뉴멕시코, 콜로라도,
유타, 아이다호 및 오레곤.

📖 **15** Read the Korean letters and use the clues to work out the meaning
of the following words:

🔊 **02.05**

a Words Korean borrowed from English and other languages:
카메라 – 메일 – 테킬라 – 레몬 –카레

b Chemical elements and compounds: 네온 – 니켈 –
메테인

c Countries and a US state: 바레인 – 레바논 –
라이베리아 – 메인

d Cities: 몬테레이 – 아테네 – 엘에이 –메카

e Famous revolutionary: 레닌

✎ **16** From the place names in 15 c and d, which place would you like to visit?

REVIEW

Here are all the letters you have learnt so far:

Consonants:

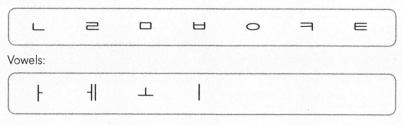

ㄴ ㄹ ㅁ ㅂ ㅇ ㅋ ㅌ

Vowels:

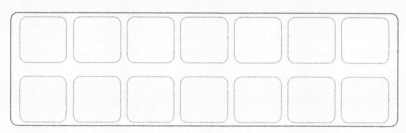

ㅏ ㅔ ㅗ ㅣ

✏ **1** Copy the letters and write the letter names underneath them.

📖 **2** A Korean woman living in the UK is inviting these people to her birthday party. Who are they?

엠마

케빈

베티

메리

킴

레나

3 FLAT LAND AND MOUNTAINS

EU —

This Korean vowel does not have a direct equivalent in English. The closest sound is the short **OO** in *good*.

#ScriptHack

The Korean letter **EU** is a single horizontal line, representing the flat ground.

In Korean, **EU** is often used as an in-between sound in order to make consonant clusters in foreign words more pronounceable, since Korean itself doesn't have many consonant clusters. For example, *cream* is spelt **keurim** in Korean, because Korean doesn't have a **kr** consonant cluster.

Below are some examples of how **EU** looks combined with some consonants.

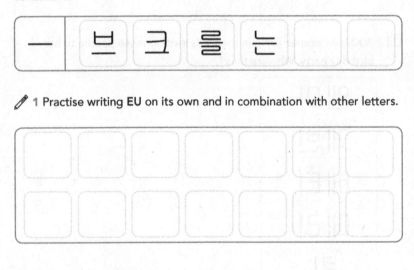

🖉 **1** Practise writing **EU** on its own and in combination with other letters.

2 Find the eight **EU**s in the following paragraph.

저는 인도네시아, 베트남, 중국, 한국, 그리고 일본이 정말 즐거웠습니다. 일본 스시와 차는 정말 맛있었습니다!

3 Read the Korean letters and use the clues to work out the meaning of the following words.

◁)) 03.01

a Names: 마이크 – 마크 – 오마르 – 카르멘

b Middle Eastern countries: 이라크 – 카타르 – 아랍에미리트

c Other countries: 크로아티아 – 아르메니아 – 베트남 – 마르티니크 – 에리트레아

d Cities: 브레멘 – 베를린 – 텔아비브 – 몬트리올 – 라바트

e German philosopher: 칸트

f Chemical elements: 코발트 – 브로민 – 크립톤

g Words borrowed from English or Scottish: 케이크 – 크림 – 킬트

Siot ㅅ

This is the equivalent of the letter **S** in Korean. It normally sounds like **S**, but in front of **I** it sounds like **SH**, hence the letter name is

 #ScriptHack

In order to remember the shape, think of **Siot** as representing the **s**ummit of a mountain.

pronounced as **shiot**. As with all Korean consonants, the Korean word for **Siot** is written with a **Siot** at the beginning and end. Therefore, you can tell that **Siot** is pronounced as **T** when it comes at the end of a syllable (as the third letter in a box). Here **Siot** is also shown in combination with other letters.

🖊 4 Practise writing **Siot** on its own and in combination with other letters.

🔍 5 Find the six **Siots** in the following paragraph.

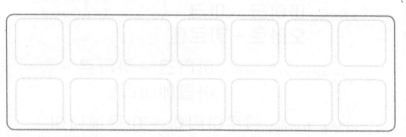

저는 인도네시아, 베트남,
중국, 한국, 그리고 일본이
정말 즐거웠습니다. 일본
스시와 차는 정말
맛있었습니다!

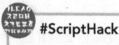

#ScriptHack

Ignore what looks like two **Siot** stuck together: that's another letter.

📖 6 Read the Korean letters and use the clues to work out the meaning of the following words.

🔊 03.02

LANGUAGE TIP

Remember that **Siot** is pronounced as **T** if it comes at the end of a syllable.

a Continents: 아시아 – 오세아니아

b Countries in Europe: 오스트리아 – 세르비아 – 슬로바키아 – 슬로베니아 – 에스토니아 – 보스니아

c Other countries: 시리아 – 이스라엘 – 오스트레일리아 – 코스타리카 – 사모아 – 미크로네시아

d American states: 미네소타 – 테네시 – 아칸소

e Places in Russia: 시베리아 – 민스크 – 옴스크 – 모스크바

f Major cities: 오사카 – 브리스톨 – 리스본 – 오슬로

g Food: 스테이크 – 토스트

h Technology: 로봇 – 로켓 – 미사일

i Music and dancing: 삼바 – 살사 – 스카

Digeut ㄷ

#ScriptHack

Digeut looks like a lowercase, square **d**, but without the stick on the right.

This is the unaspirated version of **Tieut** ㅌ. An aspirated letter, like the English **T**, is pronounced with a puff of air which you can feel when you put your hand a short distance in front of your mouth, while an unaspirated letter, like the English **D**, does not have this puff of air. In Korean, the distinction is important, and there is a series of letters that exist in an aspirated and unaspirated version. The aspirated Korean letter will then usually have one extra line compared to the unaspirated version (the unaspirated is considered to be the base form). You can see this with aspirated **Tieut** ㅌ and unaspirated **Digeut** ㄷ. **Digeut** is transliterated as **d**, because it is unaspirated like the English letter **D**, even though it's not a perfect equivalent of **D**.

Here **Digeut** is also shown in combination with other letters.

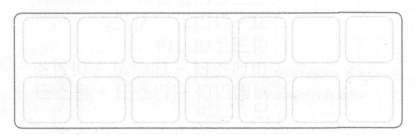

| ㄷ | 다 | 디 | 도 | 담 | | |

🖊 **7** Practise writing **Digeut** on its own and in combination with other letters.

🔍 **8** Find the seven **Digeuts** in the following paragraph.

새로운 친구들을 사귀고 진짜
재미있었습니다. 저희는 볼링도 쳤습니다.
오랜만에 여행해서 좋았지만 이제 집에
돌아와서 기쁘기도 합니다.

📖 **9** Read the Korean letters and use the clues to work out the meaning of the following words.

◁)) **03.03**

a Names: 아담 – 돈 – 오드리 – 에디 –
블라디미르

b Words borrowed from English: 카드 – 디스크 –
비디오

c Countries: 인도네시아 – 캄보디아 – 마케도니아 – 덴마크 – 아이슬란드 – 안도라

d Former British colony: 인도

e Cities that were part of this colony: 마드라스 – 다카 – 이슬라마바드

f European cities: 로테르담 – 암스테르담 – 드레스덴 – 마드리드 – 톨레도

g Places in the USA: 네바다 – 콜로라도 – 노스다코타 – 디트로이트

h Drinks: 보드카 – 레모네이드

i Famous people: 마돈나 – 살바도르 달리 – 달라이 라마 – 넬슨 만델라

10 Here are some movie genres whose names are the same in Korean. Work out how to spell them in Hangul: *indie, comedy, drama*.

Pieup ㅍ

 #ScriptHack

Pieup looks like the Greek letter **pi**.

This is the aspirated version of **Bieup** ㅂ, equivalent to the English letter **P**, which is also aspirated in English. In foreign words, **Pieup** is also often used in place of the letter **F**, for which Korean has no equivalent.

Here **Pieup** is also shown in combination with other letters.

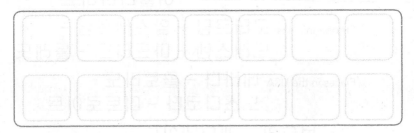

| ㅍ | 파 | 프 | 포 | 필 | | |

✎ **11** Practise writing **Pieup** on its own and in combination with other letters.

| | | | | | |
| | | | | | |

🔍 **12** Find the three **Pieups** in the following paragraph.

아프리카에서는 에티오피아, 모잠비크,
그리고 이집트가 특히 좋았습니다. 카이로는
너무 복잡했고, 사하라는 너무 더웠지만,
나일강과 피라미드들은 정말 아름다웠습니다.

📖 **13** Read the Korean letters and use the clues to work out the meaning of the following words.

◁)) 03.04

a European cities: 파리 – 소피아 – 안트베르펜 –
벨파스트

b States and cities in the USA: 미시시피 –
펜실베이니아 –
플로리다 – 멤피스 –
필라델피아

c European countries: 스페인 – 폴란드 – 키프로스 – 핀란드

d Other countries: 파키스탄 – 네팔 – 파나마 – 에티오피아 – 필리핀

e Somewhere to go in the evening: 파티

f What you might find there: 파스타 – 팝콘 – 펩시 – 스프라이트

g Words Korean borrowed from English: 피라미드 – 테이프

✏ **14** Here are two more words that Korean borrowed from English: *caffeine* and *asphalt*. Write them in Hangul using the letters you already know.

U ㅜ

This is the equivalent of the letter **U** in Korean, pronounced as the long **OO** in *boot*. It consists of a horizontal line (the earth / the horizon) with a dot or short line (sun) below it.

#ScriptHack

Remember **U** as representing sundown.

U is a wide vowel, like **O**, so this is how it fits into syllables:

| ㅜ | 푸 | 쿠 | 순 | 풀 |

✏ **15** Practise writing **U** on its own and in combination with other letters.

[writing practice grid]

🔍 **16** Find the four Us in the following paragraph.

많은 주들을 봤습니다: 뉴욕, 매사추세츠, 뉴저지, 아칸소, 오클라호마, 뉴멕시코, 콜로라도, 유타, 아이다호 및 오레곤. 새로운 친구들을 사귀고 진짜 재미있었습니다.

📖 **17** Read the Korean letters and use the clues to work out the meaning of the following words.

◁》 03.05

   a Korean and Asian cities: 뭄바이 – 푸네 – 부산 – 울산 – 쿠알라룸푸르

   b Middle Eastern cities: 두바이 – 아부다비 – 베이루트 – 카불 – 무스카트 –이스탄불

   c American countries: 페루 – 쿠바 – 베네수엘라 – 온두라스 – 수리남 – 푸에르토리코

d African countries: 수단 – 부룬디 – 카메룬 – 부르키나파소 – 코트디부아르

e North American peoples: 수 – 이누이트

f Currency: 파운드

g Foods: 쿠스쿠스 – 브라우니 – 두부

18 Which of the places in 17 a–d would you like to visit?

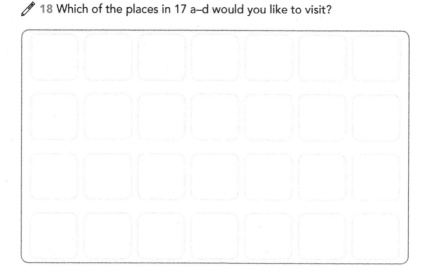

REVIEW

Here are all the letters you have learnt so far:

Consonants:

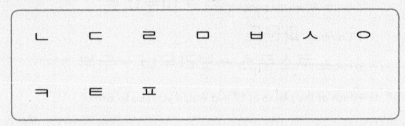

Vowels:

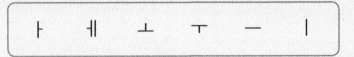

🖉 1 Copy the letters and write the letter names underneath them.

📖 2 Read the names of these famous thinkers and artists.

코페르니쿠스

엘비스 프레슬리

파블로 피카소

살바도르 달리

카를 마르크스

아리스토텔레스

4 G AND VOWELS WITH Y AND W

Giyeok ㄱ

This is the equivalent of the letter **G** in Korean. It's the unaspirated version of **Kieuk** ㅋ, so you can remember it because it has one less

#ScriptHack

In order to remember the shape, think of **Giyeok** as representing the basic shape of a gun.

line than **Kieuk** ㅋ. As all Korean consonants, **Giyeok** is written with the letter **Giyeok** at the beginning and end. Therefore, you can tell that **Giyeok** is pronounced as **K** when it comes at the end of a syllable (as the third letter in a box).

Like **Nieun**, **Giyeok** bends quite a bit when combined with a tall vowel, not so much when combined with a wide one:

✏ 1 Practise writing **Giyeok** on its own and in combination with other letters.

2 Find the seven **Giyeoks** in the following paragraph.

저는 인도네시아, 베트남, 중국, 한국, 그리고
일본이 정말 즐거웠습니다. 일본 스시와 차는
정말 맛있었습니다!

3 Read the Korean letters and use the clues to work out the meaning
of the following words.

◁)) 04.01

 #ScriptHack

Remember that **Siot** combined with **I** is pronounced **SHI**, not **SI**.

a Music: 레게 – 록 – 기타

b Countries in Africa: 가나 – 기니 – 토고 –
감비아 – 우간다 – 세네갈 –
마다가스카르

c Countries in Europe: 그리스 – 포르투갈 –
벨기에 – 룩셈부르크 –
불가리아 – 몬테네그로

d Korean name for the USA: 미국

e Places in the USA: 미시간 – 텍사스 – 시카고 –
피닉스

f Words Korean borrowed from English: 게임 – 피크닉 –
스파게티 – 마가린 – 박테리아 – 넥타이

g A series, and famous character: 스타 트렉 – 스폭

h Indian leader: 간디

🖉 **4** How would you write *Mexico City* in Hangul? (Use **Giyeok+Siot** for
the **x**.)

EO ㅓ

Despite the strange transliteration as
EO, the sound of this Korean vowel
comes closest to the **O** in the English
word *often*. Refer to the audio in order
to get it right.

#ScriptHack

Imagine this letter as a stick
figure with arms flapping
helplessly as it falls backwards
into the mud.

Here are some examples of how **EO** looks combined with some consonants:

| ㅓ | 버 | 퍼 | 덜 | 걱 | | |

🖉 **5** Practise writing **EO** on its own and in combination with other letters.

🔍 6 Find the four EOs in the following paragraph.

많은 주들을 봤습니다: 뉴욕, 뉴햄프셔,
매사추세츠, 뉴저지, 버지니아, 테네시,
아칸소, 오클라호마, 아이다호 및 오레곤.
저희는 정말 많은 테킬라와 위스키를
마셨습니다.

📖 7 Read the Korean letters and use the clues to work out the meaning of the following words.

◁)) 04.02

a Male names: 피터 – 크리스토퍼 – 험프리

b Cities in the British Isles: 에든버러 – 더블린 –
런던 – 리버풀

c Other English-speaking cities: 에드먼턴 – 보스턴 –
볼티모어 – 멜버른 –
털사 – 덴버

d Musical instruments and where you might hear them:
드럼 – 아코디언 – 트럼펫 – 콘서트

e Food and drink: 코코넛 – 도넛 – 커피 – 럼

f Transportation: 버스 – 트럭 – 모터

g More words Korean borrowed from English:
킬로미터 – 퍼센트 – 서비스 –
바이러스 – 다이너마이트

h Former president: 빌 클린턴

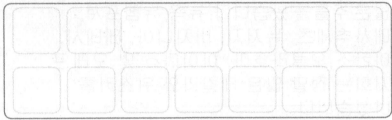

Vowels with Y

#ScriptHack

The short line represents the concept of the sun. Remember that if you see two suns, you have been drinking!

Now we'll take a huge step forward. It is important to note that Korean does not have a letter **Y**. Instead, whenever Korean needs to render **ya**, **ye**, **yo**, **yu** and so on, it doubles the short line on the vowel. For example, the Korean word for *York* is 요크, and the word for *Kyoto* is 교토. It helps that every Korean vowel naturally only has one short line. Since these double short lines don't occur naturally, doubling them is unambiguous. Whenever you see a Korean vowel with a doubled short line, it must start with **Y**:

ㅏ	a	ㅑ	ya
ㅓ	eo	ㅕ	yeo
ㅔ	e	ㅖ	ye
ㅗ	o	ㅛ	yo
ㅜ	u	ㅠ	yu

Examples of this vowel class in action:

| ㅕ | 얀 | 예 | 뉴 | 요 | 교 | |

✏ 9 Practise writing vowels with **Y**.

┌─────────────────────────────────────┐
│ ┌──┐ ┌──┐ ┌──┐ ┌──┐ ┌──┐ ┌──┐ ┌──┐ │
│ └──┘ └──┘ └──┘ └──┘ └──┘ └──┘ └──┘ │
│ ┌──┐ ┌──┐ ┌──┐ ┌──┐ ┌──┐ ┌──┐ ┌──┐ │
│ └──┘ └──┘ └──┘ └──┘ └──┘ └──┘ └──┘ │
└─────────────────────────────────────┘

🔍 10 Find the seven vowels with **Y** in the following paragraph.

많은 주들을 봤습니다: 뉴욕, 뉴햄프셔,
매사추세츠, 아칸소, 오클라호마, 뉴멕시코,
콜로라도, 유타, 아이다호 및 오레곤. 저희는
정말 많은 테킬라와 위스키를 마셨습니다.

📖 11 Read the Korean letters and use the clues to work out the meaning
of the following words.

🔊 04.03

a Chemical elements: 마그네슘 – 타이타늄 –
알루미늄 – 크로뮴 – 세슘 –
우라늄 – 플루토늄 – 리튬 –
머큐리

b Names: 나타샤 – 샤론 – 에브게니

c Food: 케사디야 – 토르티야 – 바비큐

d Alcoholic drinks: 코냑 – 셰리 – 샴페인

e Island paradises: 버뮤다 – 모리셔스 – 세이셸

f Continent: 유럽

g Cities: 리야드 – 예루살렘 – 나고야 –
뉴델리 – 뉴올리언스 – 뉴욕

h Words borrowed from English: 컴퓨터 – 메뉴 –
뉴스 – 슈퍼마켓

i Famous actor: 숀 코너리

✎ **12** The following words also use the Y sound in Korean. Write them in Hangul using the letters you already know: *Euro, judo, yoga, Maya*.

AE ㅐ

This is the last distinct Korean vowel that you haven't encountered yet. Nowadays most Koreans pronounce it in the same way as **E**, like the **E** in *bed*.

#ScriptHack

AE looks like a ladder.

This vowel also has a variant with **Y** (**yay**), with two short lines rather than one: ㅒ

Here **AE** is also shown in combination with other letters.

| ㅐ | 배 | 래 | 샌 | 맬 | | |

✎ **13** Practise writing **AE** on its own and in combination with other letters.

14 Find the seven **AE**s or **YAE**s in the following paragraph.

저희는 볼링도 쳤습니다. 오랜만에 여행해서
좋았지만 이제 집에 돌아와서 기쁘기도
합니다. 여행에 대해서 할 얘기가 많습니다.

15 Read the Korean letters and use the clues to work out the meaning
of the following words.

◁)) 04.04

  a American cities: 마이애미 – 탬파 – 샌디에고 –
신시내티 – 새크라멘토 –
시애틀 –샌프란시스코

  b UK cities: 애버딘 – 캔터베리 – 뉴캐슬 –
글래스고

  c Other English-speaking cities: 캔버라 – 애들레이드 –
캘거리 – 밴쿠버 –
오클랜드

  d Superheroes: 배트맨 – 슈퍼맨

  e Actors: 브래드 피트 – 맷 데이먼

  f Words borrowed from English: 벨리 댄스 – 랩 –
택시 – 배드민턴 –
배터리 – 킬로그램

  g Something colourful to eat: 샐러드

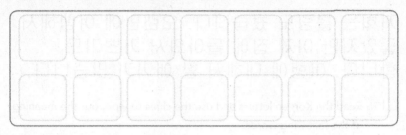

More diphthongs

The final part of this lesson is about the last Korean diphthongs that you haven't encountered yet. Diphthongs are complex vowel sounds, where two vowel sounds are combined together in the same syllable, such as the diphthong **AI** in the English word *pain*, which is different from the simple **A** vowel in *pan*. The following further combinations are possible. When the standard transliteration is surprising, it has been marked in bold.

Combinations with **O**:

Hangul	ㅘ	ㅙ	ㅚ
Letters	o+a	o+ae	o+i
Transliteration	wa	wae	**oe**

Combinations with **U** and **EU**:

Hangul	ㅝ	ㅞ	ㅟ	ㅢ
Letters	u+eo	u+e	u+i	eu+i
Transliteration	**wo**	we	wi	ui

The combination always consists of a wide vowel and a tall vowel; it's impossible to combine two wide vowels or two tall vowels, if only because that would cause difficulty in writing.

To fit a diphthong into the imaginary square, the distribution of letters will always look like this:

Consonant	Tall vowel
Wide vowel	

Or with a final consonant:

Consonant	Tall vowel
Wide vowel	
Final consonant	

Some practical examples:

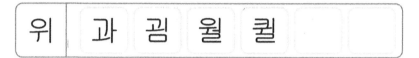

위 과 굄 월 퀄

✏️ **17** Copy the diphthongs out below.

🔍 **18** Find the four diphthongs in the following paragraph.

카이로는 너무 복잡했고, 사하라는 너무
더웠지만, 나일강과 피라미드들은 정말
아름다웠습니다. 유럽에서 저는 많은
박물관들을 방문했습니다.

📖 19 Read the Korean letters and use the clues to work out the meaning of the following words.

🔊 04.05

a Names: 위니 – 다윗 – 에드워드 – 윌리엄

b Food and drink: 위스키 – 퀴노아 – 과카몰리

c European countries: 스웨덴 – 스위스 – 노르웨이

d Latin American countries: 과테말라 – 에콰도르 –
파라과이 – 우루과이 –
니카라과

e Cities: 오타와 – 위니펙 – 밀워키 –
튀니스 – 뒤셀도르프 – 쾰른

f A part of the UK: 웨일스

g Famous writers: 마크 트웨인 – 괴테

h Korean borrowings from America: 스퀘어 댄스 – 퀼트

✏️ 20 How would you spell *Taekwondo* in Hangul? (Use **G** instead of **K**.)

REVIEW

Here are all the letters you have learnt so far:

Consonants:

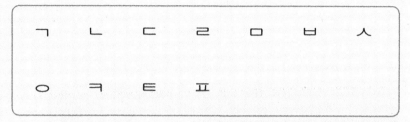

Vowels:

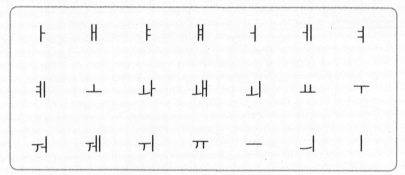

The vowel collection is now complete.

✏ **1 Copy the letters and write the letter names underneath them.**

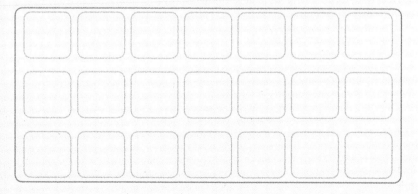

✏️ **2** What does it say on the sign in Hangul? Copy it out.

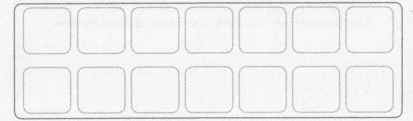

5 LAST CONSONANTS

Jieut ㅈ

This is the Korean equivalent of the English **J** as in *jungle*. At the end of a syllable, the pronunciation changes to **T**, as you can see from the letter name.

 **#ScriptHack**

The letter **Jieut** looks like a stick figure jumping.

Here **Jieut** is also shown in combination with other letters.

ㅈ	저	조	집	즐	

✏️ **1** Practise writing **Jieut** on its own and in combination with other letters.

🔍 **2** Find the five **Jieuts** in the following paragraph.

저는 인도네시아, 베트남, 중국, 한국, 그리고 일본이 정말 즐거웠습니다. 일본 스시와 차는 정말 맛있었습니다!

📖 3 Read the Korean letters and use the clues to work out the meaning of the following words.

🔊 05.01

a Names: 조 – 제인 – 아이작 – 제임스 – 제니 – 잭 – 존 – 줄리아

b Cities: 리우데자네이루 – 자카르타 – 조지타운 – 로스앤젤레스

c Countries: 이집트 – 자메이카 – 타지키스탄 – 나이지리아 – 짐바브웨 – 뉴질랜드

d Food and drink: 오렌지주스 – 주키니 – 피자 – 라자냐

e Famous singers: 마이클 잭슨 – 믹 재거 – 존 레논

f Words borrowed from English: 엔진 – 메시지 – 이미지 – 텔레비전

#ScriptHack

When foreign words are spelt with a **Z**, in Korean you'll usually find **Jieut**, because Korean doesn't have the **Z** sound.

✏️ 4 The fifth largest city in South Korea, with a population of more than 1.5 million, is Daejeon. Write this city name in Hangul.

Hieut ㅎ

This is the equivalent of the letter **H** in Korean. Depending on the font, the top will either be a short horizontal line or a dot that connects with the lower horizontal line.

#ScriptHack

Think of **Hieut** as a face (circle) wearing a **h**at.

Here **Hieut** is also shown in combination with other letters.

ㅎ	해	한	호	헬

✏️ 5 Practise writing **Hieut** on its own and in combination with other letters.

🔍 6 Find the eight **Hieuts** in the following paragraph.

미국에서 제 친구 마크와 저는 해안에서
해안까지 도로여행을 했습니다. 많은 주들을
봤습니다: 뉴욕, 뉴햄프셔, 버지니아,
오클라호마, 뉴멕시코, 유타, 아이다호 및
오레곤.

📖 7 Read the Korean letters and use the clues to work out the meaning of the following words.

◁)) 05.02

a Names: 해리 – 헬레나 – 하산 – 무함마드

b Places for a beach holiday: 하와이 – 바하마 – 타히티 – 호놀룰루

c European towns and cities: 코펜하겐 – 함부르크 – 스톡홀름 – 하노버 – 핼리팩스

d American states: 오하이오 – 아이다호 – 오클라호마 – 뉴햄프셔

e The name of South Korea in Korean: 대한민국

f Words borrowed from English: 하우스 – 호러 – 햄버거 – 호텔 – 할라페뇨

g Famous singer and actress: 휘트니 휴스턴

✏ **8** A famous Korean car manufacturer is Hyundai. Write this name in Hangul. It uses **AE** as the final vowel.

leung ○

You have already learnt **leung** as the placeholder consonant for syllables that actually start with a vowel. Interestingly, **leung** can also be used at the end of a syllable, and then it produces an **NG** sound as in *going*.

 #ScriptHack

leung ends in **NG**, which confirms the rule that you can tell how a letter sounds at the start or end of a syllable by looking at the letter name.

Here **leung** is shown at the end of syllables in combination with other letters.

✎ 9 Practise writing **leung** on its own and in combination with other letters.

🔍 10 Find the two **leungs** used at the end of a syllable in the following paragraph.

📖 11 Read the Korean letters and use the clues to work out the meaning of the following words.

◁)) 05.03

    a Chinese cities: 홍콩 – 상하이 – 베이징 – 난징 – 광저우

    b Other cities: 방콕 – 앙카라 – 카사블랑카 – 킹스턴 – 버밍엄 – 워싱턴

    c Countries: 헝가리 – 방글라데시 – 콩고 – 싱가포르 – 프랑스 – 몽골

    d The UK, in Korean: 영국

e Rivers: 라인강 – 템스강 – 볼가강 – 나일강

f American leaders: 에이브러햄 링컨 – 마틴 루터킹

g Words borrowed from English: 펭귄 – 망고 – 빌딩 –
쇼핑 – 탱크

LANGUAGE TIP

River names in Korean always end in 강 (*river*).

📖 12 How do you say *Stop* in Korean, according to this sign?

✏️ 13 How would you spell *Pyongyang (Pyeongyang)* and *Samsung
(Samseong)* in Korean?

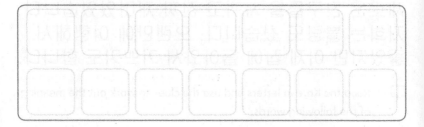

Chieut ㅊ

This is the aspirated version of **Jieut** ㅈ,
as you can guess because it has one
more line than **Jieut**. It sounds closer to
CH than to **J**. It also tends to replace **TS**
in foreign words. **Chieut** is transliterated
as **ch** normally, or as **t** at the end of a
syllable, as per the usual pattern.

#ScriptHack

Either think of **Chieut** as
Jieut with an extra line for
aspiration, or imagine it as
representing a stick figure
doing Tai **Chi**.

Here **Chieut** is also shown in combination with other letters.

| ㅊ | 차 | 츠 | 초 | 첸 | |

🖊 **14** Practise writing **Chieut** on its own and in combination with other letters.

🔍 **15** Find the three **Chieut**s in the following paragraph.

또한 모차르트, 바흐, 차이코프스키를
들었습니다. 미국에서 제 친구 마크와 저는
해안에서 해안까지 도로여행을 했습니다.

📖 **16** Read the Korean letters and use the clues to work out the meaning
of the following words.

🔊 05.04

a Asian cities: 카라치 – 첸나이 – 청두

b Other cities: 리치먼드 – 로체스터 –
맨체스터 – 크라이스트처치

c Countries: 보츠와나 – 차드 – 체코 – 칠레

d Food: 체리 – 샌드위치

e Words borrowed from English: 채팅 – 마이크로칩 –
치와와 – 스포츠카 –
비치발리볼

f Famous composers: 차이코프스키 – 모차르트

g Famous leaders: 체 게바라 – 칭기즈 칸 –
원스턴 처칠

📖 **17** This food is known as **kimchi** in the Western world. What is it called in Korean?

Tense consonants

Five of the Korean consonants can also be pronounced in a 'tense' way, achieved by tensing / stiffening up your vocal tract. Writing these consonants is simple: you simply write the base letter twice. In the standard transliteration, these letters are rendered as **kk**, **tt**, **pp**, **ss** and **jj**.

The letter names are **Ssang-Giyeok**, **Ssang-Digeut**, **Ssang-Bieup**, **Ssang-Siot** and **Ssang-Jieut**.

✏️ **18** Practise writing the tense consonants.

🔍 **19** Find the six tense consonants in the following paragraph.

새로운 친구들을 사귀고 진짜 재미있었습니다.
저희는 볼링도 쳤습니다. 오랜만에 여행해서
좋았지만 이제 집에 돌아와서 기쁘기도
합니다.

📖 **20** Read the Korean letters and use the clues to work out the meaning
of the following words.

🔊 05.05

    a Asian city: 호찌민 시
    b Communist leader: 마오쩌둥
    c Something that you chew: 껌
    d Religious text of Islam: 꾸란
    e Sound of a gun: 빵
    f Dad: 아빠

📖 **21** The tense letters are typically Korean, so they don't often appear in
cognates. Practise them some more by noting down the
transliteration of the following Korean words and phrases.

Hangul	Transliteration	Meaning
꽃		*flower*
토끼		*rabbit*
꿀		*honey*
딸기		*strawberry*
땅콩		*peanuts*
쌀		*rice*
딸		*daughter*

Hangul	Transliteration	Meaning
아저씨		*uncle*
쌍둥이		*twins*
첫째		*first*
골짜기		*valley*
안녕하십니까?		*How are you?*
몇 살입니까?		*How old are you?*
따뜻합니다.		*It is warm.*
예쁘군요.		*She is pretty.*
끝냅시다.		*Let's finish.*

22 Write the name of the Korean car manufacturer Ssangyong in Hangul.

REVIEW

You have now learnt all the Korean letters. The following is the traditional alphabetical order, which is used in dictionaries.

Consonants:

Vowels:

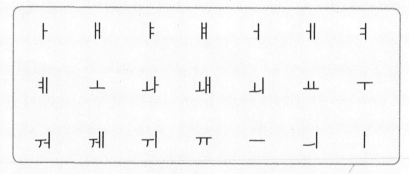

✏ **1** Copy the letters and write the letter names underneath them, then memorize this order.

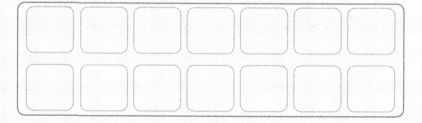

📖 **2** Transliterate as many as possible of the Korean shop names and billboards in the picture. Some words will be familiar, others not.

6 **DIFFERENT WRITING STYLES**

Like all scripts, Hangul can be written in many different fonts and writing styles. As Korean is traditionally written with a brush, a basic difference lies in how well the font shows the varying thicknesses and the crookedness of brushstrokes vs. the even, straight lines of a digital representation.

한글 vs. 한글 vs. 한글

Nowadays most Koreans use pens of course, and modern handwriting may look like this:

한글

Of course there are also bombastic, pixelated and other situation-appropriate fonts, as in English.

한글
한글

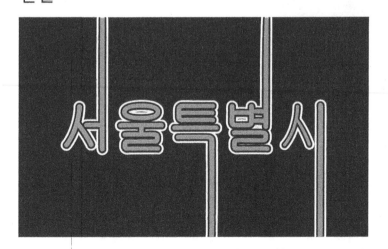

Most Korean, especially on the computer or in print, is written in the form we have used in this course. You'll get used to the other forms, especially handwriting, through regular exposure to Korean.

📖 **1** Read the following names of great writers in handwriting:

헤밍웨이, 셰익스피어, 제인 오스틴,
마크 트웨인

📖 **2** Write the transliteration of this bar name.

📖 **3** What is the name of South Korea's national day in Korean?

National Liberation
Day of Korea

광복절
8.15

REVIEW

📖 1 Transliterate this handwritten phrase, which means 'How are you?' in Korean.

안녕하십니까 ?

✏️ 2 Copy the above twice: the first time, try to imitate this handwritten style as closely as you can. The second time, use standard letters such as you have learnt throughout the course.

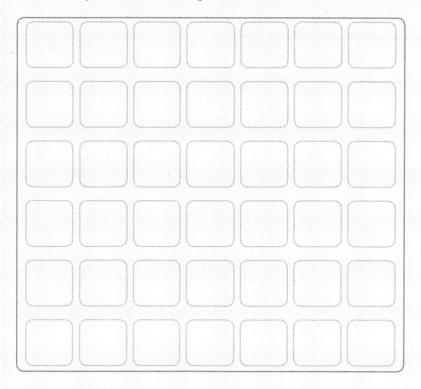

Congratulations, you have reached the end of this course!

To be able to read Korean novels or newspapers, you will still have to learn the language itself. However, you can already do a lot. Tick the things you can do:

☐ I can read and pronounce the Korean alphabet.

☐ I can read the names of streets or shops.

☐ I can read people's names on their business cards.

☐ I can recognize brands at the shop.

☐ I can spot English words when they masquerade as Korean.

☐ I know how to spell the names of dishes at a Korean restaurant.

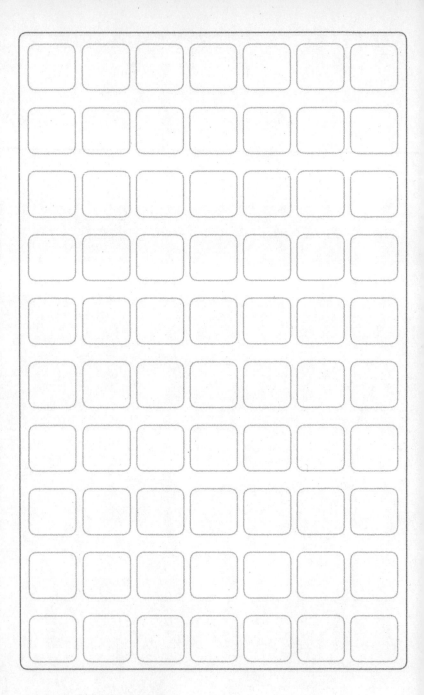

ANSWER KEY

Lesson 1

The highlighted areas throughout the answer key show the Korean letters in their syllable boxes, so you get used to seeing how they most commonly appear. Sometimes, you'll find more than one of the letters you're looking for in a box.

2 저는 인도네시아, 베트남,
중국, 한국, 그리고 일본이
정말 즐거웠습니다.
일본 스시와 차는 정말
맛있었습니다!

5 저는 인도네시아, 중국, 한국, 그리고 일본이
정말 즐거웠습니다.

7 저는 인도네시아, 베트남, 중국, 한국, 그리고
일본이 정말 즐거웠습니다. 일본 스시와 차는
정말 맛있었습니다!

8 **babara**, meaning *Barbara*

10 저는 인도네시아, 베트남, 중국,
한국, 그리고 일본이 정말
즐거웠습니다. 일본 스시와
차는 정말 맛있었습니다!

11 a **bil** = *Bill*, **billi** = *Billy*

   b **rira** = *Lira*

   c **ril** = *Lille*

13 저는 인도네시아, 베트남, 중국, 한국, 그리고 일본이 정말 즐거웠습니다. 일본 스시와 차는 정말 맛있었습니다!

14 a **aba** = *Abba*

  b **ribia** = *Libya*

  c **alli** = *Ali*

16 저는 인도네시아, 베트남, 중국, 한국, 그리고 일본이 정말 즐거웠습니다. 일본 스시와 차는 정말 맛있었습니다!

17 a *banana*

  b *Anna*, **nil** = *Neil*

  c *Iran, Albania*

  d **abana** = *Havana*

  e **bin** = *Vienna*

  f **banilla** = *vanilla*

Review

2

Korean	Transliteration	Meaning
알	**al**	*egg*
비	**bi**	*rain*
반	**ban**	*half*

Lesson 2

From now on, if a Korean word is spelt almost the same as in English, the solutions will only provide the English.

2 저는 인도네시아, 베트남,
중국, 한국, 그리고 일본이
정말 즐거웠습니다. 일본
스시와 차는 정말
맛있었습니다!

3 a *Maria*

b *Namibia, Mali*

c *Amman, Manama*

d *Manila*, **rima** = *Lima*

e *Annam*

f **ma-il** = *mile*

g **bab malli** = *Bob Marley*

5 뉴욕, 뉴햄프셔, 매사추세츠, 뉴저지,
버지니아, 테네시, 아칸소, 오클라호마,
뉴멕시코, 콜로라도, 유타, 아이다호 및
오레곤.

6 a *Naomi, Noah*

b **roma** = *Rome*, **millano** = *Milan, Bonn*

c *Nairobi*

d *Illinois*

e **bollibi-a** = *Bolivia, Oman*

f **ilbon**

g **ba-i-ollin** = *violin*

8 뉴욕, 뉴햄프셔, 매사추세츠, 뉴저지, 버지니아,
테네시, 아칸소, 오클라호마, 뉴멕시코,
콜로라도, 유타, 아이다호 및 오레곤.

9 a *Kim*

   b *Morocco, Monaco, Colombia,* **komoro** *= Comoros Islands*

   c *Cairo, Colombo, Macao*

   d *Nokia, Coca Cola*

   e *icon, cocoa, kilo, alcohol*

11 그리고 톨스토이, 셰익스피어, 괴테, 쉴러, 칼
   마르크스에 대해 배웠습니다. 또한 모차르트,
   바흐, 차이코프스키를 들었습니다.

12 a *Tom, Tony,* **matin** *= Martin*

   b *Toronto, Quito, Kolkata, Tallinn, Almaty,* **torino** *= Turin, Antananarivo*

   c **itallia** *= Italy,* **molta** *= Malta,* **aiti** *= Haiti,* **moritani** *= Mauritania*

   d *taco*

   e **bitamin** *= vitamin*

14 많은 주들을 봤습니다: 뉴욕, 뉴햄프셔,
   매사추세츠, 뉴저지, 버지니아, 테네시,
   아칸소, 오클라호마, 뉴멕시코, 콜로라도,
   유타, 아이다호 및 오레곤.

15 a *camera,* **me-il** *= mail, tequila,* **remon** *= lemon,* **kare** *= curry*

   b *neon, nickel,* **mete-in** *= methane*

   c *Bahrain, Lebanon,* **ra-iberi-a** *= Liberia,* **me-in** *= Maine*

   d *Monterrey,* **atene** *= Athens, LA (Los Angeles), Mecca*

   e *Lenin*

Review

2 *Emma, Kevin, Bettie, Mary, Kim, Lena*

Lesson 3

2 저는 인도네시아, 베트남, 중국, 한국, 그리고 일본이 정말 즐거웠습니다. 일본 스시와 차는 정말 맛있었습니다!

3 Keep in mind that often the **EU** will be silent in the English word.

a **ma-ikeu** = *Mike*, **makeu** = *Mark*, **omareu** = *Omar*, **kareumen** = *Carmen*

b *Iraq, Qatar,* **arabemiriteu** = *United Arab Emirates (UAE)*

c *Croatia, Armenia,* **beteunam** = *Vietnam*, **mareutinikeu** = *Martinique, Eritrea*

d *Bremen,* **bereullin** = *Berlin*, **telabibeu** = *Tel Aviv*, **monteuriol** = *Montreal, Rabat*

e *Kant*

f *cobalt, bromine,* **keuribton** = *krypton*

g **keikeu** = *cake*, **keurim** = *cream, kilt*

5 저는 인도네시아, 베트남, 중국, 한국, 그리고 일본이 정말 즐거웠습니다. 일본 스시와 차는 정말 맛있었습니다!

6 a *Asia,* **ose-ani-a** = *Oceania*

b **oseuteuri-a** = *Austria, Serbia, Slovakia, Slovenia, Estonia, Bosnia*

c *Syria, Israel,* **oseuteure-illi-a** = *Australia, Costa Rica, Samoa, Micronesia*

d *Minnesota, Tennessee,* **akanso** = *Arkansas*

e *Siberia, Minsk, Omsk,* **moseukeuba** = *Moscow*

f *Osaka,* **beuriseutol** = *Bristol*, **riseubon** = *Lisbon, Oslo*

g **seute-ikeu** = *steak*, **toseuteu** = *toast*

h *robot, rocket*, **misa-il** = *missile*

i *samba, salsa, ska*

8 새로운 친구들을 사귀고 진짜
재미있었습니다. 저희는 볼링도 쳤습니다.
오랜만에 여행해서 좋았지만 이제 집에
돌아와서 기쁘기도 합니다.

9 a *Adam, Don*, **odeuri** = *Audrey, Eddie*, **beulladimireu** = *Vladimir*

   b **kadeu** = *card, disk*, **bidi-o** = *video*

   c *Indonesia, Cambodia, Macedonia, Denmark*, **a-iseullandeu** = *Iceland, Andorra*

   d **indo** = *India*

   e *Madras (Chennai), Dhaka, Islamabad*

   f *Rotterdam, Amsterdam, Dresden, Madrid, Toledo*

   g *Nevada, Colorado*, **noseudakota** = *North Dakota*, **diteuro-iteu** = *Detroit*

   h *vodka*, **remone-ideu** = *lemonade*

   i *Madonna, Salvador Dali, Dalai Lama, Nelson Mandela*

10 인디, 코미디, 드라마

12 아프리카에서는 에티오피아, 모잠비크,
그리고 이집트가 특히 좋았습니다. 카이로는
너무 복잡했고, 사하라는 너무 더웠지만,
나일강과 피라미드들은 정말 아름다웠습니다.

13 a *Paris*, **sopi-a** = *Sofia*, **anteubereupen** = *Antwerp*, **belpaseuteu** = *Belfast*

   b *Mississippi*, **pensilbe-ini-a** = *Pennsylvania*, **peullorida** = *Florida*, **mempiseu** = *Memphis*, **pilladelpi-a** = *Philadelphia*

c **seupe-in** = *Spain, Poland,* **kipeuroseu** = *Cyprus,* **pinrandeu** = *Finland*

d *Pakistan, Nepal, Panama, Ethiopia,* **pillipin** = *Philippines*

e **pati** = *party*

f *pasta,* **papkon** = *popcorn, Pepsi,* **seupeura-iteu** = *Sprite*

g *pyramid,* **te-ipeu** = *tape*

14 카페인, 아스팔트

16 많은 주들을 봤습니다: 뉴욕, 매사추세츠,
뉴저지, 아칸소, 오클라호마, 뉴멕시코,
콜로라도, 유타, 아이다호 및 오레곤. 새로운
친구들을 사귀고 진짜 재미있었습니다.

17 a *Mumbai, Pune, Busan, Ulsan,* **ku-allarumpureu** = *Kuala Lumpur*

b *Dubai, Abu Dhabi, Beirut, Kabul, Muscat, Istanbul*

c *Peru, Cuba,* **benesu-ella** = *Venezuela, Honduras, Suriname, Puerto Rico*

d *Sudan, Burundi, Cameroon,* **bureukinapaso** = *Burkina Faso,* **kuteu dibu-areu** = *Côte d'Ivoire*

e **su** = *Sioux, Inuit*

f **pa-undeu** = *pound*

g *couscous,* **beura-uni** = *brownie,* **dubu** = *tofu*

Review

2 The names: *Copernicus, Elvis Presley, Pablo Picasso, Salvador Dali, Karl Marx, Aristotle*

Lesson 4

2 저는 인도네시아, 베트남, 중국, 한국, 그리고
일본이 정말 즐거웠습니다. 일본 스시와 차는
정말 맛있었습니다!

3 a *reggae, rock,* **gita** = *guitar*

   b *Ghana,* **gini** = *Guinea, Togo, Gambia, Uganda, Senegal, Madagascar*

   c **geuriseu** = *Greece, Portugal,* **belgi-e** = *Belgium,* **ruksembureukeu**
      = *Luxembourg, Bulgaria, Montenegro*

   d **miguk**

   e **mishigan** = *Michigan,* **teksaseu** = *Texas,* **shikago** = *Chicago,*
      pinikseu = *Phoenix*

   f **ge-im** = *game, picnic, spaghetti, margarine, bacteria,* **nekta-i** = *necktie*

   g **seuta teurek** = *Star Trek,* **seupok** = *Spock*

   h *Gandhi*

4 멕시코시티

6 많은 주들을 봤습니다: 뉴욕, 뉴햄프셔,
   매사추세츠, 뉴저지, 버지니아, 테네시,
   아칸소,오클라호마, 아이다호 및 오레곤.
   저희는 정말 많은 테킬라와 위스키를
   마셨습니다.

7 a **piteo** = *Peter,* **keuriseutopeo** = *Christopher,* **heompeuri** = *Humphrey*

   b **edinbeoreo** = *Edinburgh,* **deobeullin** = *Dublin,* **reondeon** =
      London, **ribeopul** = *Liverpool*

   c *Edmonton, Boston,* **boltimo-eo** = *Baltimore,* **melbeoreun** =
      Melbourne, Tulsa, **denbeo** = *Denver*

   d *drum,* **akodi-eon** = *accordion,* **teureompet** = *trumpet,* **konseoteu** =
      concert

   e *coconut, doughnut,* **keopi** = *coffee, rum*

   f *bus, truck (lorry),* **moteo** = *motor*

   g *kilometre,* **peosenteu** = *per cent,* **seobiseu** = *service,* **ba-ireoseu** =
      virus, **da-ineoma-iteu** = *dynamite*

   h *Bill Clinton*

8 서울

10 많은 주들을 봤습니다: 뉴욕, 뉴햄프셔, 매사추세츠, 아칸소, 오클라호마, 뉴멕시코, 콜로라도, 유타, 아이다호 및 오레곤. 저희는 정말 많은 테킬라와 위스키를 마셨습니다.

11 a *magnesium*, **ta-itanyum** = *titanium, aluminium, chromium, caesium, uranium, plutonium*, **rityum** = *lithium*, **meokyuri** = *mercury*

b *Natasha*, **syaron** = *Sharon*, **yebeugeni** = *Yevgeni*

c *quesadilla, tortilla*, **babikyu** = *barbecue*

d **konyak** = *cognac*, **syeri** = *sherry*, **syampe-in** = *champagne*

e *Bermuda*, **morisyeoseu** = *Mauritius*, **se-isyel** = *Seychelles*

f **yureop** = *Europe*

g *Riyadh, Jerusalem, Nagoya, New Delhi*, **nyu-olli-eonseu** = *New Orleans*, **nyu-yok** = *New York*

h **keompyuteo** = *computer, menu*, **nyuseu** = *news*, **syupeomaket** = *supermarket*

i **syon koneori** = *Sean Connery*

12 유로, 유도, 요가, 마야

14 저희는 볼링도 쳤습니다. 오랜만에 여행해서 좋았지만 이제 집에 돌아와서 기쁘기도 합니다. 여행에 대해서 할 얘기가 많습니다.

15 a **ma-i-ae-mi** = *Miami, Tampa*, **saendi-ego** = *San Diego, Cincinnati, Sacramento, Seattle*, **saenpeuransiseuko** = *San Francisco*

b *Aberdeen, Canterbury*, **nyukaeseul** = *Newcastle*, **geullaeseugo** = *Glasgow*

c   *Canberra,* **aedeullae-ideu** = *Adelaide, Calgary,* **baenkubeo** =
    Vancouver, **okeullaendeu** = *Auckland*

d   *Batman, Superman*

e   *Brad Pitt, Matt Damon*

f   *belly dance, rap, taxi, badminton, battery, kilogram*

g   **saelleodeu** = *salad*

16 캐나다, 알래스카

18 카이로는 너무 복잡했고, 사하라는 너무
   더웠지만, 나일강과 피라미드들은 정말
   아름다웠습니다. 유럽에서 저는 많은
   박물관들을 방문했습니다.

19 a   *Winnie,* **dawit** = *David,* **edeuwodeu** = *Edward, William*

b   *whisky, quinoa, guacamole*

c   *Sweden,* **seuwiseu** = *Swiss = Switzerland, Norway*

d   *Guatemala, Ecuador, Paraguay, Uruguay, Nicaragua*

e   *Ottawa, Winnipeg,* **milwoki** = *Milwaukee, Tunis,* **dwiseldoreupeu** =
    Düsseldorf, **koelleun** = *Cologne (Köln)*

f   **we-ilseu** = *Wales*

g   *Mark Twain, Goethe*

h   **seukwe-eo daenseu** = *square dance, quilt*

20 태권도

Review

2   **Seoul yeok** (**yeok** = *station*)

Lesson 5

2 저는 인도네시아, 베트남, 중국, 한국, 그리고 일본이 정말 즐거웠습니다. 일본 스시와 차는 정말 맛있었습니다!

3 a Joe, **je-in** = Jane, **a-ijak** = Isaac, **je-imseu** = James, Jenny, Jack, John, Julia

b Rio de Janeiro, Jakarta, **jojita-un** = Georgetown, **roseu-aenjelleseu** = Los Angeles

c **ijipteu** = Egypt, Jamaica, Tajikistan, Nigeria, Zimbabwe, **nyujillaendeu** = New Zealand

d **orenjijuseu** = orange juice, **jukini** = zucchini (courgette), **pija** = pizza, **rajanya** = lasagne

e **ma-ikeul jaekseun** = Michael Jackson, Mick Jagger, John Lennon

f engine, **mesiji** = message, **imiji** = image, **tellebijeon** = television

4 대전

6 미국에서 제 친구 마크와 저는 해안에서 해안까지 도로여행을 했습니다. 많은 주들을 봤습니다: 뉴욕, 뉴햄프셔, 버지니아, 오클라호마, 뉴멕시코, 유타, 아이다호 및 오레곤.

7 a Harry, Helena, Hassan, Muhammad

b Hawaii, Bahamas, Tahiti, Honolulu

c Copenhagen, Hamburg, Stockholm, **hanobeo** = Hannover, **haellipaekseu** = Halifax

d **oha-i-o** = Ohio, Idaho, Oklahoma, **nyuhaempeusyeo** = New Hampshire

e **Daehanminguk**

f **ha-useu** = *house*, **horeo** = *horror*, **haembeogeo** = *hamburger*, *hotel*,**hallapenyo** = *jalapeño*

g **hwiteuni hyuseuteon** = *Whitney Houston*

8 현대

10 새로운 친구들을 사귀고 진짜 재미있었습니다. 저희는 볼링도 쳤습니다. 오랜만에 여행해서 좋았지만 이제 집에 돌아와서 기쁘기도 합니다.

11 a *Hongkong, Shanghai, Beijing, Nanjing*, **gwangjeo-u** = *Guangzhou*

   b *Bangkok, Ankara, Casablanca, Kingston*, **beomingheom** = *Birmingham, Washington*

   c *Hungary, Bangladesh, Congo, Singapore*, **peurangseu** = *France*, **monggol** = *Mongolia*

   d **yeongguk**

   e **ra-ingang** = *Rhine river*, **temseugang** = *Thames river*, **bolgagang** = *Volga river*, **na-ilgang** = *Nile river*

   f **ae-ibeureohaem ringkeon** = *Abraham Lincoln*, **matin ruteo king** = *Martin Luther King*

   g *penguin, mango, building*, **syoping** = *shopping*, *tank*

12 jeong ji

13 평양, 삼성

15 또한 모차르트, 바흐, 차이코프스키를 들었습니다. 미국에서 제 친구 마크와 저는 해안에서 해안까지 도로여행을 했습니다.

16 a *Karachi, Chennai, Chengdu*

   b **richimeondeu** = *Richmond, Rochester, Manchester*, **keura-iseuteucheochi** = *Christchurch* c **bocheuwana** = *Botswana, Chad*, **cheko** = *Czechia / Czech Republic, Chile*

d *cherry, sandwich*

e *chatting, microchip, chihuahua*, **seupocheuka** = *sports car*, **bichiballibol** = *beach volleyball*

f **cha-ikopeuseuki** = *Tchaikovsky*, **mochareuteu** = *Mozart*

g *Che Guevara*, **chinggijeu kan** = *Genghis Khan, Winston Churchill*

17 gimchi (김치)

19 새로운 친구들을 사귀고 진짜 재미있었습니다. 저희는 볼링도 쳤습니다. 오랜만에 여행해서 좋았지만 이제 집에 돌아와서 기쁘기도 합니다.

20 a **hojjimin si** = *Ho Chi Minh City*

b **ma-ojjeodung** = *Mao Tse-tung*

c *(chewing) gum*

d *Quran*

e *bang*

f **appa** (similar to *papa*)

21

Hangul	Transliteration	Meaning
꽃	kkot	flower
토끼	tokki	rabbit
꿀	kkul	honey
딸기	ttalgi	strawberry
땅콩	ttangkong	peanuts
쌀	ssal	rice
딸	ttal	daughter

Hangul	Transliteration	Meaning
아저씨	ajeossi	*uncle*
쌍둥이	ssangdungi	*twins*
첫째	cheotjjae	*first*
골짜기	goljjagi	*valley*
안녕하십니까?	annyeonghasimnikka?	*How are you?*
몇 살입니까?	myeot sarimnikka?	*How old are you?*
따뜻합니다.	ttatteuthamnida.	*It is warm.*
예쁘군요.	yeppeugunyo.	*She is pretty.*
끝냅시다.	kkeutnaepsida.	*Let's finish.*

22 쌍용

Review

PhotoStudio on the left, and again on the Fujifilm sign: **wonsajingwan**

Second building from the right: **motel**

Next to 'MASSAGE': **masaji**

Restaurant underneath 'MASSAGE': **chikinbaengi**

Lesson 6

1 *Hemingway, Shakespeare, Jane Austen, Mark Twain*

2 **Maekjuchanggo**

3 **Gwangbokjeol**

Review

1 annyeonghasimnikka? (The combination **Bieup-Nieun** is pronounced *mn* due to assimilation.)

PHRASEBOOK

🔊 06.01

Hello	**Annyeonghaseyo**	안녕하세요
Hi	**Annyeong**	안녕
Excuse me	**Sillehamnida**	실례합니다
Welcome	**Hwanyeonghamnida**	환영합니다
How are you?	**Eotteoke jinaesimnikka?**	어떻게 지내십니까?
Fine, thank you	**Jal jinaemnida, gamsahamnida**	잘 지냅니다, 감사합니다
Nice to meet you	**Mannaseo ban-gapseumnida**	만나서 반갑습니다
Please	**Butakhamnida**	부탁합니다
Thanks	**Gomapseumnida**	고맙습니다
You're welcome	**Cheonmaneyo**	천만에요
Here you are	**Yeogi Ittseumnida**	여기 있습니다
I'm sorry	**Joesonghamnida**	죄송합니다
I don't understand	**Moreugetseumnida**	모르겠습니다
Do you speak English?	**Yeongeoreul hasimnikka?**	영어를 하십니까?
Yes / No	**Ye / Aniyo**	예 / 아니요
Goodbye	**Annyeonghi gaseyo**	안녕히 가세요

PHOTO CREDITS

p58 © Ki young / Shutterstock.com

p64 © Zoart Studio / Shutterstock.com

p66 © Banana Walking / Shutterstock.com

p70 © SAHACHATZ / Shutterstock.com

p71 © GrAl / Shutterstock.com

p72 © Kelli Hayden / Shutterstock.com

p72 © vso / Shutterstock.com